ADDICTIVE SERVICE

UNLEASH YOUR POTENTIAL

KURT FELDNER

Book Design by Aeyshaa

Paperback - 979-8-9854902-0-6
Ebook - 979-8-9854902-1-3

Publisher: Kurt Feldner
krfeldner@gmail.com
kurtfeldner.com
Submit special orders by email

TABLE OF CONTENTS

INTRODUCTION:

ABOUT ME

I've been actively involved in service-related work pretty much all my life. So really, I've been – and still am – in your shoes.

As a 13-year-old, I had my first job, which was working for the local Dairy Queen, serving ice cream and related goodies. After that, I worked for another ice cream store (hey, I admit, I LOVE ice cream), followed by working at two different airports, refueling general & commercial aviation aircraft. After that, I transitioned into the insurance industry, processing life, disability and medical claims, issuing policies, processing policy loans, setting up investment accounts, and numerous other functions, all of which included assisting clients on the phone, as well as in correspondence and emails. And to boot, I'm a voice over artist, providing the voice for audiobooks, radio commercials, videos, on-hold phone recordings/ phone trees, etc.

I've been married to my beautiful wife, Cindi going on 38 years & we have two grown children, Wes & Katie. Between their two families, we have 7 grandchildren. In addition to being passionate about customer service, I also love working in the yard, construction-related projects inside and outside the home, power tools (Tim The Toolman...you're my hero), traveling to and vacationing in tropical destinations (give me a beach and palm trees and I'm a happy guy), camping, brewing and sampling a variety of coffees, eating ice cream, and following sports, especially college and professional football. Growing up in Ohio, I followed the lead of my parents and became a life-long fan of the Cincinnati Bengals, Cincinnati Reds and THE Ohio State Buckeyes (both of our kids, as well as my daughter-in-law all graduated from OSU). Outside of work and family, I've also served for years on the board of directors for a non-profit organization that helps kids learn how to grow and develop healthy relationships, and have also served for many years in our local church in areas such as the media team, community outreach projects, small groups, choir and a coffee ministry.

And lastly, I would like to give thanks to my early role models and inspirations in showing me how to be a servant – my parents, Richard and Paula Feldner. My dad had that quiet and selfless attitude, always gentle, smiling and serving our family and those around him. And my mom, who served our family with incredible love, and who's gift of hospitality just naturally translated into serving others. And over the last 30+ years, I've seen my wife serve our kids, grandkids and those she manages with a love and deep passion that is unmatched. And last – but definitely not least – I'm thankful to God, who placed this gift of service in my heart.

CHAPTER 1

THE REASON WHY

Over the past several years, I've come to notice the level of service in restaurants and stores has dropped below what I consider acceptable levels. Many of the men and women who serve us are in a J-O-B, simply looking for a paycheck. You know... back in the day, we would always anticipate and usually receive a smile and greeting – something along the lines of, "Hello! Welcome to XX. How may I help you today?" Or if on a phone call, something like, "Hello. Thanks for calling XX. How may I assist you today?"

Not long after a recent Christmas, my wife and I were having breakfast on a Saturday morning at a well-known pancake restaurant. Our server looked at us with what appeared to be a forced and faint smile, asked what we wanted and took our order, then headed to the kitchen. I told my wife, "Hardly anyone any more seems to know how to deliver good customer service. I just wish there was something I could do to help." She looked at me and said, "You know...you ought to author a book on the subject of customer service. You're passionate about customer service and you're an excellent writer." I looked at her and said, "Hmmm." I'd never even given consideration to writing a book about the subject. I told her I'd give it some thought.

A couple of weeks later, I said to my wife, "You remember that conversation we had when I told you I wished there was something I could do to help improve customer service, and you suggested I author a book on the subject?" She said, "Yes." I continued, "Well, I've been thinking about that ever since and after really thinking it through, I think I will take you up on your suggestion. I'm going to go ahead and write a book." She had a large smile on her face and said, "Oh good!" I further commented, "Yep, and I even have a name for the book. Do you want to know what it is?" She said, "Sure!" I said, "Okay, the name of the book is going to be, "<u>Addictive Service</u>." I could see the gears turning in her mind as she contemplated the words. She thought about it for a moment and said, "Oh....I get it! You provide such great service that people will want to keep coming back to you - because they're addicted to it!" I paused for a moment and said, "Hmm...that's a great way to interpret it, but that's not really what I had on my mind when I came up with the title. What I was thinking was...people who are really passionate about serving find that they're addicted to it and need to keep doing so because they feel so good when doing it." I told her it seems her thoughts about the title, as well as mine, BOTH accurately fit the title of the book.

Within a week, I had purchased the web domain, "AddictiveService.com" and was ready to begin writing the book.

CHAPTER 2

THE SIMPLE MEANING

T he Merriam Webster dictionary defines "serve/serving/served" as:

- To be a servant

- To assist

- To be of use

- To be favorable, opportune, or convenient

- To be worthy of reliance or trust

- To prove adequate or satisfactory

As you can see from the above definitions, serve or serving is a verb – a word of *action*.

It's not an "is," but a "does."

It "transfers." It starts with me and transfers to you.

CHAPTER 3
FIGURING OUT WHY I SERVE

When I entered the customer service arena, I wasn't job searching with the goal of getting a position that involved service. I was looking for a job in a smaller town than where my previous job was located and the options were much more limited. The job I ended up taking was in a brand-new field to me, and part of the responsibilities included serving the customer on the telephone and in letters. Adjudicating disability claims was the primary responsibility. Serving the customer was necessary in my job description, though it was viewed more as a secondary function. I served the customer because I HAD to – it was just part of the job.

I eventually moved on to other companies and positions and all involved serving customers, with some placing more emphasis than others on this role. Through all these roles, I served the customer – mainly because it was part of the job description. I didn't protest, but honestly, I didn't serve with a passion either. Yet....all the while it did seem "natural" for me to be serving. I never consciously examined my motives for serving, but just "did it." Perhaps you're in a job or situation like that right now?

It's okay to serve in auto-pilot mode, as long as you fulfill the responsibilities your employer has in engaging and serving the customer. But at some point, you need to realize your job can be SO MUCH MORE life-altering for you AND the customer if you tap into your potential. That's when serving begins to be fun. You see, when you begin to have fun with serving, that's really when it starts to become... addictive.

CHAPTER 4

I'M A CUSTOMER TOO

We serve who? The customer. What we sometimes forget is – we are a customer too. For example, you subscribe to utility services for your home or apartment – you're their customer. You pay your mechanic to fix your car – you're the customer. You get your hair cut or styled at the barbershop or salon – you're their customer. You buy yourself some new clothes – you're the customer. You work out at the gym – you're the customer. You make regular purchases with your favorite online merchant or retailer – you're the customer. You eat out at your favorite restaurants – once again, you're the customer.

When you act as the customer, what are your expectations at the time of the sale or service? Are you okay with minimal interaction? What if the employee acts indifferent and seems as if they could care less that you're patronizing them? Does that bother you? What if the employee on the other end of the phone talks in a monotone, disinterested voice? What if every time you visit the gym it seems like a fourth of the machines have an "out of order" sign on them because the machines need repaired? (The latter is an example of indirect customer service and will be discussed more in the next chapter.) Do any of these things get under your skin?

ALL of the above examples should cause you to feel like you're receiving less than what you deserve.

Because you're a customer too, you can easily identify how you feel when you're regarded as an afterthought.

Take mental notes as you go throughout your day – notice how you're treated as the customer. Pay attention to the things that bother you, things that make you feel like you're being cheated out of great service. Begin to make a *mental list* of the things you should remember NOT to do when you're serving. Breathe a short verbal "reminder" statement out loud, "I will NOT do (insert whatever negative service issue you take affront to)." If you're around others and you don't want them to think you're crazy because they hear you talking to yourself, mumble softly that statement, but you definitely want to verbalize it to help it sink in.

CHAPTER 5

INDIRECT CUSTOMER SERVICE – AKA: THE PATH

Serving the customer is more than words. It's more than bringing food to their table. It's more than a smile on your face or a friendly, "How can I help you?" There's an indirect path to serve that may or may not be within your control, but it helps to better understand that path. Even if your responsibilities are not on that path, you can help *influence the path's direction.*

Consider all the things that a customer encounters when they visit or have an encounter with your business, whether in person or on the phone.

1. How's the temperature of the room or building? If it's too hot or too cold, a negative feeling is formed immediately – yes, even before the direct service is performed.

2. How are the products displayed? Are they easy to see or reach?

3. How long does the customer wait while on hold?

4. Is your phone tree/on-hold system cumbersome and complicated?

5. Does your phone tree/on-hold system sound *friendly & helpful?*

6. If your business includes equipment that helps fulfill what the customer needs or wants, it needs to work. If it's broken down, your job of serving just gets that much more challenging.

7. How comfortable are those chairs in the restaurant, or on a bus or airplane?

There are so many more examples that aren't even listed here. The important thing to know about these and other examples is...even though some of them may be out of your direct control, you should always be searching for ways you can get your feelings heard at the level where some of these decisions are being made. If you become committed – and addicted – to the total quality service path – customers will choose that path first before considering your competitor.

CHAPTER 6
EXTERNAL AND INTERNAL CUSTOMERS

Everyone – even those who don't consider themselves to be in a service role know and understand what an external customer is. The external customers are the people that you serve who aren't in your group, organization, or employer. That seems pretty clear. But what's an *internal* customer? The internal customer is someone who works or interacts with you within your group, organization or employer.

An internal customer is VERY important to the success of your organization, because you're all on the same team and your corporate success hinges on how well you *serve each other*. LET ME REPEAT THIS – your corporate success hinges on how well you serve each other.

Maybe your internal customer is bogged down and it's looking questionable if they will be able to meet their deadline. You can step in and offer assistance. Greet them at the beginning of the day or a shift with a nice smile and "hello," and ask how they're doing. You need to regularly interact and engage with them. Also, as you know, responsibilities are sometimes shared by multiple areas. Don't drop the ball on your shared role. Instead, attack it with the heart of a servant. If everyone within the organization operates in this fashion, I can tell you - special things will begin to happen.

My wife works for a well-known regional insurance company. Her company came up with an idea to present the "MAX Service Award" to associates who go above and beyond normal service boundaries. Associates are nominated by their peers and management if they're found to be putting into practice outstanding service to external AND internal customers. This employer realizes they must serve each other if they're going to be successful in the marketplace. And the MAX Service Award reinforces the CRITICAL importance of this.

Adopt the mindset of unilateral service to ALL who cross your path.

CHAPTER 7

LOCKING IN ON THE LANGUAGE

Language seems to always be in flux. New phrases come into use and old ones slip away. Some for the better, some for the worse.

Let's look at a few words and phrases that have been around for generations, as well as some newer ones that have taken their places. Some of the newer words and phrases should be removed from a service provider's vocabulary when handling a customer's needs – others might be more of my own personal preference – and I can explain why.

When your customer thanks you for your service, I've heard the service provider use these responses:

- "Sure"

- "Uh huh"

- "No problem"

- "Of course"

All of the above examples are great in personal conversation. But they seem at best, very casual, and at worst, lackadaisical and disinterested in the professional world. The, "no problem" one is what really gets to me, as it seems to suggest a scenario where the customer's request for service is a problem to the service provider. The service provider should never give the impression that they're not there for any other reason than to serve the customer. A customer's request should never be portrayed as a potential problem.

My suggestion for a response to a customer who's thanking you would be:

- "You're welcome"

- "My pleasure"

Both of these responses are time-tested, courteous and speak to the effort and purpose of why the server is there in the first place. If you've ever been to a Chick-fil-A restaurant, you know that, "My pleasure" is always the response their workers are trained to use. It actually seems so rare to hear that phrase in places of business that one night when my wife and I were having dinner at a Red Lobster restaurant, our server used that phrase several times that evening. Upon returning to our table, I asked her, "Did you ever work at a Chick-fil-A restaurant?" Her response was, "no," saying she never worked there. I went on to explain why I asked. She said she is asked that question often, and that using that phrase is just something she ENJOYS DOING. Needless to say, we had a great experience that night and felt like our server connected with us. She made us feel as if she was there to truly serve and make our dining experience as enjoyable and pleasant as it could possibly be.

Here's another example of language that has changed – or should I say, has been removed. Think about when you're completing a transaction, whether you're placing an order at a fast-food restaurant, or buying your weekly groceries. You give the service worker your money, they hand you a receipt and then...they say, "Have a good day." Let me say, I DO appreciate them wishing me a good day. But if you're paying attention, you're seeing more and more service providers seem to be forgetting one VERY important and critical two-word response – THANK YOU. PLEASE be sure to say, "thank you" before saying, "Have a good day."

And lastly, when your sale or transaction is completed, please do not say, "Have a good one." The English language continues to be mauled more and more these days. And this is just one prime example. This phrase is popular among millennials. But remember this....not all customers are in that same age class. Use a phrase that's familiar and appreciated by ALL age classes – "Have a good day." *Always speak a language that relates to the broadest audience possible.*

CHAPTER 8

SERVING THE CUSTOMER WITH THE KEYBOARD

Most don't think of customer service when it comes to a pen or keyboard. The usual context of customer service is either in-person or over the phone. But think about the service reps who are responsible for answering emails or letters, or are involved in an online chat assistance forum. The writing element brings a unique perspective because the rep and the customer can't gauge facial reactions, or hear the tones in each other's voices. That makes written service all that more challenging.

There are two categories we'll cover in this chapter: 1) Language. 2) Timeliness.

When you're communicating with a customer in a letter, email or online chat, avoid the exclamation marks and words in all caps. Both convey a sense of shouting or yelling, and can sometimes be interpreted as condescending. Keep the tone friendly and respectful. Greet the customer with a "thanks for reaching out to us." And follow up with a, "I'm happy to help you with..." OR "I'm happy to help answer your question." Finish up the email with a, "Let (us/me) know if you should have any (other) questions."

When I first learned how to write letters, my manager reviewed every one of my letters (not emails) for a year or more. Yes, for over a year! It seemed to get ridiculous with the amount of red pen markups she used. Most of the markups were related to brevity. She kept hammering home the point that it's important to use as few words as possible, yet still get the point across. That wisdom still holds true today, and even more so with emails. Emails are intended to be short and brief.

And finally, one of the most important things to know about emails is the customer's expectation of response time. If the customer wasn't concerned about time, they would drop a letter in the mail to you. But because they're reaching out by email instead, they're expecting a quicker response. From the time I first began responding to customer's emails, here's the response timeframes I chose to follow:

1. The customer's email comes in during the morning – they have a response back by EOB (end of business) that day.

2. The customer's email comes in during the afternoon – they have a reply by EOB the next day.

The above are goals and are not ironclad. Your workload will be heavier some days and it may take a little longer to respond. But if you find yourself consistently taking more than the above times to reply, I'd say you and your manager need to figure out a workaround to your workload. A fast response time must be a top priority for emails. Even if you can't get a complete answer right away, acknowledge the email with a quick reply and let them know you're looking into the matter and will have an answer very shortly. Stay in touch with the customer every day or two until you have the answer or solution to their original question or comments. Customers want to be sure you haven't forgotten about them.

CHAPTER 9
THAT RUDE AND OBNOXIOUS CUSTOMER

Most of my customer service experience has been phone-based. I've had my share of rude, obnoxious and demanding customers in telephone conversations. But of course, you encounter them in face-to-face situations as well.

No matter whether you're serving in a face-to-face or over the phone encounter, there's a reason why the customer is angry and/or rude. That behavior is more often than not something they've carried with them for a while. They dole it out to family, friends and those they don't personally know. You need to know - it's not personal – it's not directed at you. Keep that at the forefront of your mind as you serve them.

Many years ago, I figured I would begin imagining those rude customers as children. Seriously. I would try to imagine them as a child. I would imagine what that rude customer must have looked like as a young boy or girl. In those early days. They were largely innocent lives at those young ages. So as I imagine those early lives, I recognize that who they are today may not be who they were as children. I interact with them today as adults – yet try and visualize them as innocent and impressionable children. I'm not talking to them in a child-like way, but instead I am looking at them with a heart of understanding and compassion.

When the customer attacks you, it's the continuation and escalation of fears and insecurities they've dealt with for a long time. It's possible they may not feel like they deserve kindness. Show them they DO deserve kindness, just as we ALL do. You're a servant, not a judge.

CHAPTER 10
THE ART OF LISTENING

Sometimes I feel like this is one of those "presents" that we all have the opportunity to unwrap, but we ignore it. We push it aside in favor of the other presents that are much more flashy, glitzy and glamorous. It does seem more exciting to open the presents that contain the elements of *talking* instead of the ones that contain the skill of *listening*.

From the time we're babies, our parents teach and instruct us in how to talk. Later, we move on to school so we can learn and grow in knowledge. During that time, our teachers are helping us to improve in our speaking and talking. But think about it....as a student, did you ever have a class in school that taught you how to listen? Did your grade card ever show, "Listening 101" or, "The basics of listening?" Is it no wonder that we have such inadequate listening skills, when all those years the message was always about learning how to talk.

Verbal communication is in large part lopsided, heavily favoring talk. The balance is extremely uneven. So my charge to you is this. If you want to be a good communicator, if you want to know, understand and connect with those you're serving, you must begin to force yourself to listen – it needs to be a major emphasis.

When we're always talking, the conversation is going in the direction WE want it to go. It's all one-sided. We end up losing out on so many opportunities to turn an average conversation into a fantastic one. In the process, we shortchange the customer big-time. We treat them as a means to an end.

When I'm at a restaurant or a store and I watch the server go on and on about this and that, when he asks me very few questions, when she barely takes a breath between words, I know this isn't someone who's there to serve. They're there for a paycheck.

Reposition yourself – do a new thing - listen more and talk less. As you practice this more and more, you'll no doubt surprise yourself with all that you're learning in the process. And most of all, the customer will realize you're there to serve, aid and assist. Not sell, avoid or ignore.

CHAPTER 11
BLAME THE MICROWAVE

I've said this for years. I blame our fast-paced, gotta-have-it-now mentality – on the microwave. That helpful electric appliance has revolutionized our way of life. Instant need, desire & want.

I remember when this oven started raising consumer's eyebrows. The thought of not having to wait 30 minutes to 2 hours to eat a meal or snack was so tantalizing. All you had to do now was open & close the door, push a few buttons, and within seconds you were now ready to satisfy your appetite. Incredible!

The idea that a microwave oven could allow your appetite to be satisfied faster has spilled over into pretty much anything and everything we do now. We have instant oil-change places and instant oatmeal. Few people grill now with charcoal briquettes when you can have instant heat with propane. Why drive to the library for your books when you can download the electronic versions in seconds? The list goes on and on. It's truly endless the ways in which we've sped up all the things we do. Patience is for losers – speed is for winners. Instant gratification wins the day.

Speed and a fast-paced lifestyle can bring negative results as well. Cutting in front of another driver to get somewhere faster shows we care more about us and less about them. That fast-paced lifestyle also fosters living in the tree-tops. When you're living in the tree-tops, you see the action above, but miss out on what's down below. You aren't seeing the full picture.

Slow down. Stop the frenetic pace and really look around you. And listen. Listen. Listen. Listen. There are opportunities to provide service that you're likely missing day after day, minute by minute. As you begin to intentionally move slower, you'll start to see things in a totally new light. You'll hear things you haven't heard before. You'll begin to connect more with those around you. And this is one of THE most important elements in delivering addictive service – being aware of the other person, focusing on them and serving their needs. You can't do this if you're always speeding by them in an absolute blur.

CHAPTER 12

THE GLOW OF THE CHARCOAL BRIQUETTE

You may or may not be familiar with the charcoal briquette. Long before propane grills came on the scene, there was the charcoal grill. And the fuel for a charcoal grill is – the charcoal briquette. What amazes me about the charcoal briquette is how the color, temperature and appearance changes from "prior to use" to "in use." Before use, the briquette is subdued, cold, and unattractive. However, once ignited, it slowly begins to change. As the contents of the briquette begin to burn, the color begins to change from black to gray and even orange. You'll even see occasional flames on and between the briquettes as the temperature heats up. As the briquette is put into action, warmth begins to be evident. No longer cold, this fuel now begins to become what it was meant to be when it was formed.

Did you ever think of yourself as being similar to a charcoal briquette? Unused, we lack warmth and purpose. When ignited though, we begin to fulfill why we were created.

CHAPTER 13

SETTING THE TONE

Going into work and knowing you'll be facing customers – either in person or taking their calls or answering their emails – can be daunting. It can even be outright scary at times. There will be some days you're just not in the right frame of mind to deal with people. You might have had a bad night's sleep. You may have had an argument at home, or been cut off by a rude driver on the road. You may feel emotionally drained. Well guess what. You're human. You're just like me and everyone else in the world.

As we start the work day, we won't always be in the right frame of mind to serve. Helping someone, answering their questions, resolving their issues or problems, and taking their orders? I can tell you - putting a smile on your face or in your voice will be the last thing on your mind some days.

Does this mean you can call in sick? Does this mean you can ask one of your co-workers who's in a great mood to take your workload and serve your customers?

Our work and responsibilities won't go away. Customers will always be present and won't care about your mood, or what's happened to you at home or on the road that day. How do you handle those less-than-optimal days? Here's a few ideas that will hopefully reframe things for you:

- Our emotions and outlook can sag when we lack sleep. Go to bed a little bit earlier, sleep a little bit later. I'll admit – this is one I wrestle with, because for a long time, I've viewed a day as, "How much can I enjoy in the hours I'm awake?" If I get up early and stay up late, I have that many more opportunities to enjoy the day, right? That's true – but at the same time, false. If you're running on fumes, getting frustrated and irritated easily, just how much enjoyment am I REALLY getting out of that day?

- Do you go to lunch with someone at work who's constantly negative? Do you enjoy hanging out with a group of friends who like to complain and gossip?

- Do you like to watch TV show hosts, listen to radio commentators, or follow those on social media who dish out a constant supply of negative content?

- Try adjusting all these things. Start looking for other friends who seem to rarely complain. Avoid engaging in gossip. If you hear it, walk away from it. On social media, you can do a couple of things: 1) Unfollow those who are always complaining and sharing negative content. 2) Put up a post that says you're looking for ideas on TV and radio shows that feature positive and encouraging content. Watch and see what your positive friends' responses are. Maybe they listen to podcasts or read books that are positive and motivating?

- The more you insert yourself into activities that are positive and align yourself with people who rarely complain, you'll see less and less negative or complaining thoughts racing through your mind. You'll begin to look for and quickly recognize the positive things that previously you had been totally overlooking and missing.

By doing the above, you'll be in a better state of mind and more ready to engage with and serve your customers. Your reshaped mind will also be noticed by customers as well, leading to more positive customer experiences.

A negative mind in a service provider never wins over the customer. BOTH parties end up UNHAPPY. A positive mind in the service worker sets the stage for a much better customer experience. And you BOTH end up coming away happy.

CHAPTER 14

WHY SERVE? WHAT'S IN IT FOR ME?

This has got to be the most telling and eye-opening question for a service professional. What caused me to start serving and why am I doing it? Is it the paycheck? Is it the adventure? Was I desperate for a job – any job? I heard a sermon from our pastor recently who asked this question when talking about the way we interact with and serve others: *"Are you doing it because of the passion, or because of the experience?"*

For many, many years, I served for the experience. It gave me a chance to meet a lot of people and see who was out there. I have met and talked with all kinds of people and it's really been an epic adventure all the way. I've worked with and served some pretty nice folks, as well as some rather rude ones. For a long time, I served because I was getting a paycheck every 2 weeks and that allowed me to pay the bills.

My world came crashing down on me in 2011 when I was called into the conference room and my boss, along with the head of HR, sat across from me at the table and told me my job of 23 years was being eliminated. I was one of 4 whose jobs were eliminated – all due to the financial bottom lines and not personal performance related - and was told this would be effective immediately, and it was time to pack up my stuff and leave. I realized right there that my adventure had come to an end.

We really don't take the time to think and analyze why we do certain things. My layoff put me in a position of really giving serious thought of why I served customers for all those years, and it also put me in a position of deciding – what next? Do I want to continue doing this?

That saying of, "you don't know what you're missing until it's gone" is, I think, what made the light bulb finally come on for me. I began to miss those social interactions – talking with people, listening to them describe why they were calling, hearing the, "thank you very much for your help today" at the end of the calls – I missed those things. The realization came over me....I'm good at this thing - customer service - not because it's a job, but because I LOVE serving others. I realized I needed that back in my life, in one way or another. I was a customer service junkie and realized I was addicted to this thing we call customer service

CHAPTER 15

DEFERRING TO THE GUEST SHOULD BE YOUR QUEST

I've found we all live life in one of two ways......taking care of our needs, or taking care of others' needs. Of course, we can't make it through life without taking care of our own needs, I mean....let's get real about it. But what I'm saying is there are some folks who just really seem to have a knack for serving others. It's natural for them. They love seeing others' needs met. They are happy when they know they have played a part in the solution to the need. This type of attitude is adopted when we operate with a dose of humility in our lives. When we make a conscious decision to defer to the other if it comes up for a vote.

You may have experienced people like this. They may be the ones in the group discussion who sit there, silent for a while, and then speak up after everyone else has contributed their ideas, thoughts & opinions. They may also be those people at the family potluck meals who stand off to the side and watch everyone else go through the line, filling their plates, and then after everyone has made it through the line, they fall in and fill their plate. These are the folks who make it a practice to exercise humility, to offer the place of honor to someone else and say, "you go first."

How does this mentality translate to serving your customers? If you think about it, the answer is probably more obvious than you may have realized. If our first reaction is to serve someone in a way that either makes it easier for me, or seems to suggest the outcome may be better for me, that's placing myself first. There's no humility involved here. But if I approach the interaction with the mentality that serving the customer is viewed as the greater priority, I'm adopting an attitude of humility. I'm deferring to someone other than myself. I'm deferring to the guest, which should be my quest. THIS, my fellow service providers, is the intersection where happiness lives.

CHAPTER 16

INTERVIEWS WITH CUSTOMER SERVICE SUPERSTARS

Do you ever wonder what makes a customer service superstar tick? What drives them? What makes them want to get up each day and do it all over again? Do they have some super human power that helps them get to superstar status? Do they eat something special, take a certain vitamin, or say a certain prayer each day? I had to know – do these superstars share some commonalities? Are there any consistencies that are obvious with all of these folks?

I needed a way to search for and find some customer service superstars, so I decided to share about my search on a few social media platforms, asking my followers to let me know if they have ever encountered a customer service superstar. I defined a customer service superstar with these indicators:

> * Someone who does their job like no one else.

> * Someone who has really connected with you.

> * Someone who just naturally seemed to know what you wanted and needed.

> * Maybe they know you by name, or they know what you always order.

> *They always greet you with a smile on their face or in their voice.

> * And someone whose service you just cannot forget.

I was thrilled with the responses I received! For each superstar I was referred to, I sent them what I believed to be a pretty detailed questionnaire, listing 34 questions which probed into their lives, going back to their childhood and then moving on up to the present. Not surprisingly, I did find some common threads in their answers to my questions. Here's what I found:

Family, Faith and Morals

These superstars were raised in families with 1 – 3 other siblings.

Their parents encouraged them to get a job and earn a living, yet did not recommend or suggest a particular field.

Most had parents who were very nurturing or encouraging when it came to investing time into their kids' lives.

Most had parents who were purposeful in offering praise to their children, though one respondent interestingly said it was just the opposite for her – to this day, the lack of kindness and love from her parents haunts her (perhaps this was a driving motivation to do better for herself?).

Half of the respondents had parents who were minimally social with other people, while the other half had a generous schedule of socializing with other families.

Most all respondents said their parents were very hospitable to others.

Almost all superstars had families who ate their evening meals together on a regular basis.

All of the respondents had parents who were active in Christian faith, with some more active than others.

Most superstars told me their parents strongly emphasized good morals.

Education:

Everyone graduated from high school – some with high honors. Some moved on to college, focusing on studies such as engineering, dance, English and biology. One of the respondents completed his 4-year degree.

Most told me they felt college education wasn't helpful in their future success, though a couple of folks said they wish they had started their studies sooner and/or completed their studies.

While in college, half of them said they were very social with others.

Work History:

Their first jobs, for the most part, involved limited exposure to serving others. Most stayed in those jobs for an average of two years, and they began at either minimum wage or slightly higher, and then they moved on to similar jobs with additional responsibility for approximately the same duration as their first jobs. Most respondents said their first 1 or 2 jobs did not involve serving customers. Half of the folks worked part-time jobs early on, while the other half worked full-time positions.

Most said they liked their managers.

Some mentioned they liked organizational structure and cleanliness.

Most said they loved working with customers, helping solve problems and assisting in helping the customers in making choices.

Most superstars were consistent in saying the groups of customers they worked with involved a mixture of small and large groups.

Motivation:

Here's something that most of those in the service industry can identify with: Half of the folks said they had a point where they doubted if customer service was the right field for them, but they pushed through and got to the other side of their doubts. Most said what kept them going and continuing to come back to their jobs was the positive feedback they would receive from their customers.

They said it just "seemed to make sense to be in this field" and it "came naturally."

One person told me they heard a story of someone who committed suicide, and in the final note left by the girl, she said she wished someone had smiled at her, or said, "hello." The superstar said this has stuck in her mind ever since then and she keeps coming back to how important it is in her service to others.

Purpose:

When asked what keeps these superstars getting up every day and coming back for more, some said it's their faith that leads them, some say they love to see people happy, and that they "care" about seeing their customer's needs met, and some say it's the relationships they develop over time. One superstar described it this way:

"Satisfaction, determination and drive keeps me coming back for more. Drive to get up every day to make everyone's experience the absolute best it can be, time after time. People NEED ME. People need to see smiles, need to be greeted and taken care of from start to finish, and need to feel appreciated. I need to make them feel like there is no other place for them to go for their needs."

Rude and Demanding Customers:

When I asked the superstars how they deal with rude or demanding customers, their responses were, "to be friendly but firm," use a calm and patient attitude, and not react with a similar attitude, as that will not help get to the root of the customer's issue." They continued, "I let the customers vent and express their frustration – it's a necessary and normal thing."

And more than one respondent said they "kill their customers with kindness."

Customer Feedback:

I asked the superstars if they enjoy positive feedback and being complimented by customers? 100% of the respondents agreed that positive feedback is integral in helping them stay motivated and refueling and refreshing them.

CHAPTER 17
WHAT'S YOUR LEGACY?

Most of us want to be remembered in a positive light when our time is up on earth. We're hoping for conversations like, "She was always there for me," "Whenever I had a question, he was always willing to give me his time and attention," or "My life is better because of how she impacted me."

Living life shouldn't be an accident. It should be defined with a purpose and a reason. *Even if you don't know what your purpose is at this time, that doesn't mean you are not here for a reason.* It took me a long time to figure out why I was here and what I was meant to be and do. Once that came into focus, it made all the difference in the world.

How long will it take for you to realize the value and importance of serving others? The clock is ticking, my friends. Now is the time to reframe your mind, tap into your potential, have fun, and set your service boundaries to be LIMITLESS!

Get started on your legacy now. Serve with passion, joy and purpose. Unleash your potential.

Serve like you're addicted to it!

www.ingramcontent.com/pod-product-compliance
Lightning Source LLC
Chambersburg PA
CBHW070032030426
42335CB00017B/2394